Mary Nina Walker
14, Trinity Street
Bungay, Suffolk
NR 35.   1EH.
Tel. 01986. 895350.
Bought from Besley's Books
Beccles
1. 10. 96 for £2. 80.

Making a Stenciled ABC Quilt

With Full-Size Patterns

Marie Monteith Sturmer

Dover Publications, Inc., New York

I dedicate this book to my dear friend, Marvel Ide. Marvel has 13 great-grandchildren and has made a beautiful appliqué ABC quilt for each one. When Marvel heard of my stenciled quilts, she said she wanted to make just one more ABC quilt, a stenciled one. I designed and cut the stencils for her quilt blocks, stitched a quilt top for myself, then stenciled both projects at the same time. Thank you, Marvel, for your inspiration. I would not have had the joy of doing this book if it were not for you. Marvel is many years young and still quilts a beautiful little stitch.

Copyright © 1991 by Marie Monteith Sturmer.
All rights reserved under Pan American and International Copyright Conventions.

Published in Canada by General Publishing Company, Ltd., 30 Lesmill Road, Don Mills, Toronto, Ontario.
Published in the United Kingdom by Constable and Company, Ltd., 3 The Lanchesters, 162–164 Fulham Palace Road, London W6 9ER.

Making a Stenciled ABC Quilt: With Full-Size Patterns is a new book, first published by Dover Publications, Inc., in 1991.

Manufactured in the United States of America
Dover Publications, Inc., 31 East 2nd Street, Mineola, N.Y. 11501

Library of Congress Cataloging-in-Publication Data

Sturmer, Marie Monteith.
    Making a stenciled ABC quilt : with full-size patterns / by Marie Monteith Sturmer.
        p.   cm.   —   (Dover needlework series)
    ISBN 0-486-26939-6 (pbk.)
    1. Patchwork—Patterns. 2. Stencil work. 3. Children's quilts. I. Title. II. Series.
T1835.S75   1991
    746.9′7—dc20   91-26057
                                                                                              CIP

Introduction

What could be a more meaningful gift than a baby quilt that can be used as a learning tool? This ABC quilt is that, plus a whole lot more. Used as a wall hanging, it can set the decorating theme of your child's room. Used as a bed cover, it can warm and cuddle your child, becoming a cozy companion, always there to comfort. These are more than enough reasons for you to create a stenciled ABC quilt for your own little one.

You might think that there will be a lot of work involved in this quilt, but consider the fun you could have if a group of mothers, grandmothers, aunts or cousins all worked together.

Assigning the stencil-making to several different people would make light work of it. Have you ever gone to a stenciling bee? It's great fun! Then, of course, it can be followed by a quilting bee.

Once you begin, who knows where this quilt will lead you? There are always new babies arriving. When you have exhausted your own gift-giving list, make a quilt for the church bazaar or a children's hospital. Some delighted child will love you.

Looking Back in Time

Stencil painting on fabric dates back to the early days of weaving, when stencil-painted designs were applied with vegetable dyes. In tropical countries, large fibrous leaves or thin bark were used for making the stencils, whose designs were taken mainly from nature. For thousands of centuries, the peoples of the Eastern Hemisphere practiced and refined the art of stenciling, establishing high technical standards. Throughout this region of the world, countless buildings were adorned with stenciling that completely covered walls and ceilings.

The origins of very early stencil motifs are difficult to trace, since the basis of many simple designs can be found the world over. Fascinating little geometric designs found in Pompeian mosaics can also be found in Arabian and Persian art. Many of the first American patchwork designs have their beginnings in these same ancient designs. Where did these designs truly come from? Who were the first to draw them? Did they appear simultaneously in different parts of the world? No one can say for certain.

The stenciled quilts that we know today are certainly not a new idea. In America, the stenciled quilt had its birth in the mid-1800s. At that time, Moses Eaton, Jr., an itinerant artist, was making his mark stenciling walls in the homes around the towns of Hancock and Dublin, New Hampshire. The rural housewives in the area picked up on the idea, and began to stencil their quilt tops, often borrowing stenciling ideas from the wall stencilers.

The very early stenciled quilts were "whole-cloth" quilts, painted on a single large piece of fabric. The stenciling process began in the center of the cloth and grew outwards until the full cloth was patterned with many motifs. A separate stencil was made for each part of the design, then these stencils were grouped and regrouped, never creating a perfectly balanced unit.

The stencil motifs were quite simple, sometimes almost naive. Flowers, rounded fruit and birds were favorite subjects, often inspired by costly imported chintz from England and India.

Extraordinary things happened when these stenciled quilts were hand quilted. The stitches, worked right next to the edge of the stenciled design, caused the design to puff a little, resembling appliqué. Although these quilts looked like elegant appliqué quilts, they took only a fraction of the time to make.

Rural women were burdened with unending household duties which left little time for fancy quilting projects. For this very reason, most of the stenciled quilts created in the 1820s were made by women living in remote areas. The stenciled quilt was beautiful, easy to make and demanded only a limited amount of time to complete. Although most rural women were never exposed to any form of art training, it was their creative drive that launched this impressive and fresh technique of quiltmaking.

Their enthusiasm for stenciling overflowed into other painted fabric projects, such as bed and window curtains, tablecloths and pillows. Sadly, few fragments of stenciled curtains and tablecloths remain today.

The era of the stenciled quilt lasted only a few years—from 1820 to 1835. The paints used for the stenciling, obtained from the country peddler and intended for exterior use on barns and farm implements, contained large amounts of salt, lead and iron, which literally ate away the fabric. When the women saw their lovely handiwork fading and washing away, they must have been disheartened.

Today, only about 35 documented stenciled quilts that date from the mid-1800s remain, housed in a half dozen of the best art museums across the country.

One cannot help but admire the enthusiasm and artistic ability of the women who made the early stenciled quilts. We have inherited the mechanics and know-how of making stenciled quilts from them and, with advances in technology, now have permanent fabric paints that will enable us to make stenciled quilts that will be lasting heirlooms. This, then, is just the beginning for us.

My grandson Carl with his ABC quilt.

Instructions for Stencil-Making and Painting

Materials

54 9″ × 9″ sheets of frosted Mylar
9″ × 12″ piece of plate glass with taped edges for a cutting base
#2 pencil with eraser
12″ ruler
Single-edged razor blades or utility knife
Small, sharp-pointed embroidery scissors
Masking tape
Transparent tape
Plastic lid from a butter or margarine tub to use as a palette
Terry cloth paint rags
Three ⅜″ stencil brushes
Acrylic paints: red, yellow, blue, brown, green and other colors
as desired
Shellac thinner for cleaning dry paint from the Mylar

My stencil designs for this ABC quilt are very individual in character, but they all follow some very basic stencil-making principles.

The areas between the stencil openings are called bridges. These bridges link the parts of the stencil material and act as structural bands to give the stencil strength. They also enhance the artistic impression of the design. Wide bridges give a bold and forceful feeling, while narrow bridges render a delicate and airy touch. Whatever the impression you wish to convey, you can do it with just a change in the width of the bridges. I like to stay with bridges of the same width throughout a given design to create a harmonious feeling.

Stencils are often more interesting when several colors are incorporated into the plan of the design. When using several colors, only one stencil sheet is necessary if the design is simple, with ample spacing between the stencil openings. Masking tape can be placed over adjacent stencil openings to prevent smudging. A stenciling shield made of scrap Mylar can also be used.

For more complex designs, separate stencils must be made for the different colors. Some stencilers prefer to draw only the parts of the design that will be stenciled in one particular color on the stencil material and make special registration marks to align the different colors correctly. With all the stencils I have made over the years, I have found that registration of complex designs is easier and more accurate when I trace the full stencil design onto each separate sheet of frosted Mylar. Registration is no problem when I align and superimpose the full drawing of the design each time I paint a different color.

When you begin to make your ABC quilt stencils, it will be helpful if you take each letter of the alphabet at a time and work with it as a unit. Complete all the stencils for each unit before proceeding to the next design. Group all stencils in separate folders. Be organized—it will save you time later on when you start to paint.

Tracing and Cutting the Stencils

Lay this book flat on a work space. Center a 9″ × 9″ sheet of Mylar, frosted side up, over a quilt block design and secure it with masking tape. The Mylar sheet will be the same size as the cut fabric quilt block. With the #2 pencil, trace the full block design onto the frosted side of the Mylar. Refer to the work notes on the quilt block design for the suggested number of stencil sheets. Your drawings should consist of a series of fancy openings that make allowances for the stencil bridges. Place an X in every area to be cut out. Mark the top of each stencil sheet with the letter of the alphabet and the color or colors it is to be used for.

All alphabet letters and numbers are cut with bridges. As you can see on my quilt, I have painted in the bridges to make them solid. I made a stenciling shield of a 3″ square scrap of Mylar with a 1″ cutout corner. Hold the stenciling shield on the painted edge and carefully fill in the bridge area.

Place the Mylar on the glass cutting base. Pierce the Mylar with the point of the cutting blade. Hold the blade steady and move the Mylar into the blade with the palm of the other hand. This may take a little practice. If you wish to maneuver the cutting tool, always pull the blade toward yourself. For problem shapes, make a small slit in the Mylar in the area to be cut out, then use small embroidery scissors. You will find it is much easier to cut if you hold the scissors under the Mylar when cutting a clockwise curve and on the top of the Mylar when cutting a counterclockwise curve. The small parts of the design should be cut first to keep the structural strength of the Mylar as long as possible. Cut all large shapes last. Paper or leather punches make perfect dots.

Any cutting mistakes on the Mylar can be successfully patched with transparent tape. Apply the tape to both sides of the cut. If the cut is small and the tape extends into an opening, use the cutting tool to remove the extra tape.

Brushes and Paints

The larger the stencil brush, the more paint you will need to use; the more paint you use, the harder the painting process is to control. I prefer a ¾″ stencil brush for most of my quilt stenciling projects. It may take me a little longer to paint, but I know I have everything perfectly under control.

Stencil painting is made easy with the use of acrylic (or latex) paint. Acrylic paints dry to the touch almost immediately on fabric, so stencils can be moved with caution over freshly painted areas. Because of this fast-drying aspect of acrylic paint, dirty paintbrushes should always be placed in the water jar until clean-up time.

House paint of interior or exterior quality may be used; decorator colors often give that special effect to your stenciled project. Textile craft paint in plastic jars or squeeze bottles is also an excellent choice.

Stenciling Techniques

The stencil paint applied to the fabric should penetrate the fibers, but should not ooze out on the underside. Most stencils do not have to be painted in solid to be well done or to produce a pleasing result.

Any painting mistake on fabric is hard to correct. If the mistake is in an isolated area, the paint can be removed quickly with soap and water. The fabric must be completely dry before it can be repainted. When a mistake occurs near other painted areas, and it is only a small blob, the stencil opening can be offset to include the error and the area can be repainted.

Many interesting effects can be created with a variety of painting techniques. "Pouncing" the stencil brush up and down, striking it on the flat end, creates a stippling effect.

Allowing the color of the fabric to be seen through the paint is a very acceptable technique. Shading of the design can be done in this way, leaving the sparsely painted areas for the highlights and concentrating the pouncing of the brush to cast a darker shadow. Stroking the brush across the fabric causes a series of small painted lines that often add excitement and movement to the design. Using a circular movement of the stencil brush with a steady contact on the fabric is a good way to make objects look round. I like to shape areas of shading with this technique, using a light hand and a "dirty" brush with a bit of a complementary color worked into the stencil brush while the base color is still in the brush. Using this way of mixing and blending colors often gives a three-dimensional effect. I stay away from using black for shading; it almost always gives a dull and uninteresting appearance to the colors.

Shadow effects can be created by stenciling in one color, allowing the paint to dry, then moving the stencil slightly and stenciling in a second color.

After the stenciling has been completed, details can be added with a waterproof permanent marker.

Creating your own stencil painting technique is best of all. Do a lot of experimenting before you take on a project. Once you have established a technique, stay with it to create a sense of unity throughout the project. The use of too many different techniques for a given project can be distracting.

I have had a great deal of fun experimenting with what I call stenciling props. Scouring around to find odds and ends of materials that have porous openings is like hunting for treasures. Interesting and exciting results can be achieved by stencil painting through such materials as chicken wire, window screen, extruded metal and plastic onion bags stretched in an embroidery hoop. Look around and see what you can find. Just place your "found" object over the Mylar opening of a design and paint. It may look like a beautifully woven fabric or a prized printed calico. Truly, the possibilities are unending!

Stenciling the Fabric

Use a protective covering on the work surface when stencil painting. A large, evenly worn terry bath towel works well and will also keep the fabric from moving. Center the Mylar stencil on the quilt block fabric, using masking tape to secure the work. Do not stretch the fabric.

Place a small amount of paint (½ teaspoon) on the plastic lid palette. Pull a bit of paint from this blob with the stencil brush and work the paint into the end of the brush by tapping and rotating the bristles on the palette. Test the brush on a scrap of fabric. If the paint coming off the brush is thick and dark, you have too much paint. Work the paint into the brush some more and repeat the test.

This is the most important moment in your stenciling process. You cannot stencil-paint with a loaded brush. Stencil painting is a dry-brush technique. A little paint goes a long way.

When you have the paint under control, you are ready to make your first "proof" or practice painting on a scrap piece of fabric. This proof will be dirty because of the pencil marks on the stencil. Be sure that the paint removes all traces of the graphite from the stencil. Any corrections to the stencil can be cut at this time.

Using the painting technique you have established, work the stencil brush off the Mylar into the opening of the stencil. This method prevents the paint from going under the stencil. Check the back side of the stencil for any unwanted paint before using it again.

Do not allow the paint to build up in the brush. After washing the brush, rub it vigorously into a terry-cloth paint rag to remove all moisture. There will be color changes for each stenciled block if you follow the colors of my quilt. Using a wet paintbrush would cause the paint to bleed into the fabric, creating a problem that most likely could never be corrected.

Allow all stencil painting to dry overnight. Heat-set the colors to make them more permanent by slowly ironing them with a hot dry iron. I use a cotton setting for muslin fabrics. Press the back side of the fabric first to draw the paint into the fibers, then press the front side of the painted fabric, using a pressing cloth.

When all the stencils are cut for your ABC quilt, you will have quite a library of stencils. Just think what you can do with all of them: pillows; floorcloths; curtains; dust ruffles; wall decorations including friezes, chair rails and window borders; floors; toy boxes; schoolbags; T-shirts; pinafores; sheets and pillowcases; cotton and rush woven rugs; towels; lamps; furniture; blouses; handbags; scarves; shoes; bathroom tiles; umbrellas; and more. You name it, and it can probably be stenciled.

The office copy machine is one of the biggest boons to stenciling since the craft began. Patterns can be enlarged or reduced, cut, pasted together and recopied to make border designs or allover designs. These machines are accurate and save countless hours of tracing and redrawing, leaving more time for the joy of stencil painting. If you don't have access to a copy machine at your office, check your classified directory.

Please note that it is unlawful to use copyrighted designs for profit. Always seek out permission first. Dover has a wide variety of books offering copyright-free designs that you can use for your work. Another possibility is to do your own designing. Nothing is more exciting than stenciling a design that you have created yourself.

General Instructions for Quiltmaking

I made my stenciled ABC quilt for my grandson Carl and, as you see, I personalized it with his name. You should feel free to make changes to create your own personal version of the quilt. The variations for my stenciled ABC quilt are endless. Try reversing some of the stencils to give them a different look or adding different details with a waterproof permanent marker. A change in the color of the quilt sashing or quilt blocks or a variance in the color of the stencil paint would create a distinctive quilt barely resembling mine.

Planning a harmonious color combination is essential to creating a lovely quilt. For example, a limited palette, such as a monochromatic color scheme (one color with many value and intensity changes), could be used. If the single color were red, for instance, the pineapples would be painted in a variety of shades of dark red to light pink. A red pineapple? Why not? Weaving such a color combination into all the quilt block designs would create a unique quilt.

Some other color combinations are:

Complementary: Two primary colors opposite one another on the color wheel, such as red and green.

Split complementary: Replacing one of the primary colors with the intermediate colors to each side of it to give three colors, such as red orange, red violet and green.

Double split complementary: Replacing both primary colors with adjacent intermediate colors to give four colors, such as red orange, red violet, yellow green and blue green.

Triad: Three colors evenly spaced around the color wheel, such as red, yellow and blue (the primary colors) or orange, green and violet (the secondary colors)

Analogous: Three to five colors next to one another on the color wheel, such as yellow, yellow green, green, blue green and blue.

Study the color wheel in *Fig. 1.* Different colors can be worked out for each combination by rotating the color wheel.

To make a color a tint, add the dark color to white paint; to make a color a darker shade, add its complementary color. Colors are magic; experiment with them and discover their possibilities.

Selecting the Fabric

The choice of fabric for your quilt is a very important one. Heavy, stiff fabric and lightweight, flimsy fabric should not be used in a quilt. Beautiful, tightly woven percale fabric is not a good choice either. Selecting a fabric of 120 to 160 thread count (threads per inch) will make the hand quilting much more pleasant. 100% cotton muslin and printed calico-type fabrics are easy to work with. Many quilters prefer a blend of cotton and polyester fibers because they are crease-resistant. This could be a wise choice if there is to be a sparse amount of quilting. You might also consider making a very soft and warm quilt from cotton flannel.

If plaid fabric is used, special care must be given to the cutting. Be consistent in using only certain parts of the plaid design. Striped fabric works well for the quilt sashing and borders. Used either vertically or horizontally, it always looks nicest when the corners are mitered. Small dot-printed calico fabric lets you do "waffle" quilting without marking the lines. The space between the dotted lines will be your guide for the quilting stitch.

Fig. 1. The color wheel.

Primary colors	Secondary colors	Intermediate colors
Red (R)	R + Y = Orange (O)	Y + O = Yellow Orange (YO)
Yellow (Y)	Y + B = Green (G)	Y + G = Yellow Green (YG)
Blue (B)	B + R = Violet (V)	B + G = Blue Green (BG)
		B + V = Blue Violet (BV)
		R + V = Red Violet (RV)
		R + O = Red Orange (RO)

B + O = Brown

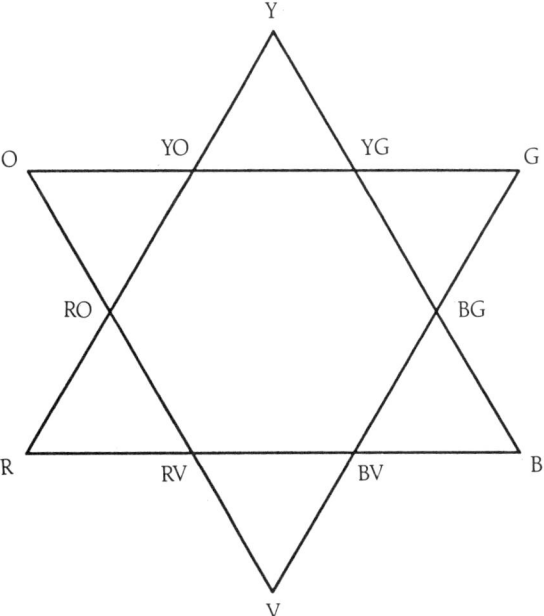

The fabric used for the top and back of the quilt should be of the same type. A printed calico used for the sashing could also be used for the quilt back.

Remember, quilting stitches are lost on printed fabric. If you have a nice quilting stitch of 8 to 10 stitches per inch, your fabric choice may be a solid color. Match the quilting thread to the fabric color.

Selecting the Batting

Batting can be made of cotton, wool or polyester bonded fibers. Of the three, polyester is by far the most functional for today's use. Polyester batting comes in several thicknesses, known as lofts. The thicker batts do not quilt well and are used for quilts that are tied with knots of yarn to hold the three layers of the quilt together. A low-loft, thin batting will enable you to make a nice small quilting stitch of up to 10 or 12 stitches per inch. These batts come in tightly rolled packages. Unwrap the batt at least two days before you are to use it so the fibers can relax.

Preparing and Cutting the Fabric

The very first step in making a quilt is to wash all fabrics to remove sizing and to press them to remove wrinkles. Trim all selvage edges. Cut all sashing and border strips from the length of the fabric first to eliminate the need to piece the borders. The quilt blocks are cut from the remaining yardage. Backing fabric and batting should be cut 3″ larger on all sides of the quilt top.

Always press the fabric as you advance from one sewing step to another, taking care not to stretch the fabric. The ¼″ seam allowances should be pressed over to one side, onto the darker fabric so shadows will not appear.

When to Stencil the Blocks

It will be a personal decision whether to paint before or after the blocks are set into the quilt top. Perhaps you are new at stenciling and a little timid. It may be well for you then to complete all the stenciling on the quilt blocks before the blocks are assembled and stitched into the quilt top. I prefer to complete all stitching on the quilt top and then stencil paint the blocks. If I do make a mistake, I remove that block and replace it with a new one. Everyone has their own way of quiltmaking and there are very few wrong ways.

Sewing the Quilt Top Together

The units of the quilt must be joined to form the quilt top. The blocks are sewn together, with or without lattice strips, to form vertical or horizontal rows, then the rows are joined. Borders are sewn to the top and bottom, then to the sides of the quilt.

Assembling the Three Quilt Layers

To assemble the quilt, place the backing fabric, right side down, on a large table (a Ping-Pong table is great). The table top should be protected from scratches. Place the batting over the backing fabric and smooth it out. Place the quilt top over the batting, right side up, and smooth it out.

Basting the three layers of the quilt together is a very important step. The basting stitches secure the quilt as a unit and keep the layers from shifting when the quilting stitches are made. Do not knot the basting threads—you may use a large back-stitch to keep the end of the thread from working loose. With a large darning needle and white thread, begin basting large stitches (1½″ to 2″ long) from top to bottom at the center of the quilt. Continue basting in rows 6″ apart, working from the center to the outer edges of the quilt until the entire top is basted. Baste a row of stitches all the way around, 1″ from the outer edges. The quilt top is now ready to receive the quilting stitches.

Quilting

The actual quilting can be done on a full-size frame, in a quilting hoop or in your lap. Which method is best is still a subject of debate among quilters, so use whichever one is most comfortable for you. I prefer to use a 14″ round adjustable quilting hoop. The quilting hoop makes quilting a transportable activity. Some say the present revival of quiltmaking was due mainly to the introduction of the modern-day quilting hoop.

Setting the quilting hoop is a major step in making a wrinkle-free quilt. Place the hoop with the screw-clamp over the place to be quilted. Place the plain wooden hoop on the underside of the quilt; smooth the quilt top and clamp the hoops together. Turn the quilt over to the back side and release the hoops carefully to smooth out the quilt back. Reclamp the hoop and return to the quilt top. Make an adjustment of the screw-clamp so the quilt will not slip when the quilting takes place. I find this very easy to do just holding the quilt on my lap. Never pull on the quilt when the hoops are clamped. Stretching can cause permanent damage to the quilt.

When resetting the hoops, always include a portion of the quilt that has already been quilted. If the quilting line extends beyond the hoop, remove the needle from the thread and rethread the needle when the hoops are moved. Do not leave the hoops in the quilt when not quilting.

Quilting needles are called betweens. The larger the number of the needle, the smaller the size of the needle. I usually work with a #8. The use of a thimble is mandatory; you will never be a good quilter without one.

The act of quilting is a mechanical procedure. As you gather stitches on your needle and draw them through the quilt, you will no longer be looking at each individual stitch as a non-quilter does. Nonquilters will often ask how you can make so many little tiny stitches. The answer is that you are not sewing individual stitches, but sewing a series of stitches at one time. This is how it is done!

Measure a thread no longer than an arm's length (18″) and cut it on a slant for easy threading. Knot one end of the thread and bring the needle into the quilt-top fabric and batting near a seam or painted edge of a stencil design where the quilting is to be worked. Pull the knot into the batting. No knots are ever left on the quilt top or back. Take a small back-stitch where the thread comes up out of the quilt to secure the thread. Place the eye end of the needle on the side or top of your thimble, whichever makes it easier to manipulate. With a rocking rhythm or an up-and-down movement of the needle and thimble, gather several stitches on the needle by going all the way through the three layers of the quilt with each stitch. The hand working under the quilt will give a slight lift to the quilt with each stitch as the needle touches (pricks) a finger. Pull the needle through to the top of the quilt and repeat. The stitches should look the same on both sides of the quilt.

If you are a beginner, don't be concerned with how many stitches you are making per inch, just concentrate on how evenly you are gathering each group of stitches. Smaller stitches will come with practice.

It is perfectly acceptable to duck and dive through the batting with the needle to get from one quilting spot to another, providing the distance is less than the length of your needle and the thread stays in the batting. Traveling threads that go from one spot to another and show on the back of the quilt are not acceptable. Do not pull these traveling threads tight.

To end off your quilting thread, take a small back-stitch where the quilting stops, send the threaded needle through the batting and come up on the quilt top a needle's length away. Cut the thread close to the top fabric.

Finishing the Quilt

The next step is to trim the batting and backing fabric even with the edge of the quilt top. Pin the binding to the right side of the quilt top, having the raw edges even. Machine-stitch the binding ¼" from the quilt top edge. Fold the binding to the back of the quilt and turn under the raw edge. Pin the binding in place, just covering the machine stitching. Hem by hand and miter the corners as you go.

Remove all basting threads. On the back of the quilt, sign your name and write down the date on which the quilt was finished and the name of the person for whom the quilt was made, using a laundry-marking pen (test it first). Or embroidery stitches can be worked over penciled letters.

Quilt Layout

2/3	A	B	C	4/5
D	E	F	G	H
I	J	K	L	M
N	O	P	Q	R
S	T	U	V	W
6/7	X	Y	Z	8/9

53″ × 62½″

Instructions for the ABC Quilt

Finished size: 53" × 62½"

Materials

44"–45" wide fabric
    3 yds. for quilt blocks and outer border
    2 yds. for sashing and binding
    3 yds. for backing
Twin size quilt batting
Sewing thread to match fabric
Quilting thread to match fabric
Embroidery thread for accents
    2 balls size 5 or 8 DMC cotton perle, green #701
    3 balls size 5 or 8 DMC cotton perle, red #321
Thimble
Sharp scissors or a rotary cutter and plastic cutting base
Watercolor fabric marker (not fast fading)
Large straight quilting pins
Large darning needle for basting
Sewing machine
14" wooden quilting hoop
Iron and ironing board
Laundry-marking pen or permanent marker for signature
Materials for stenciling the blocks (see page 7)

Cutting the Fabric

Cut two strips 49" × 2½" and two strips 63" × 2½" for outer borders. Cut 30 quilt blocks 9" × 9". Cut six strips 58½" × 1½" for vertical sashing and 35 strips 9" × 1½" for horizontal sashing. Cut two strips 65" × 3" and two strips 55" × 3" for binding. Cut the backing fabric in half crosswise.

Sewing the Quilt Together

Use ¼" seam allowance throughout. Following the quilt layout on page 12, join seven short sashing strips and six quilt blocks to make a vertical row (*Fig. 2*). Repeat to form five rows of six blocks each. Join the long sashing strips and the five rows (*Fig. 3*). Sew the short outer border strips to the top and bottom of the quilt top; sew the long outer border strips to either side (*Fig. 4, next page*).

Sew the two widths of backing fabric together along a long edge. The binding will be added after the quilt has been quilted.

Give the quilt top and quilting backing fabric one last good pressing before putting the quilt together. Assemble the three layers following the general instructions on page 10.

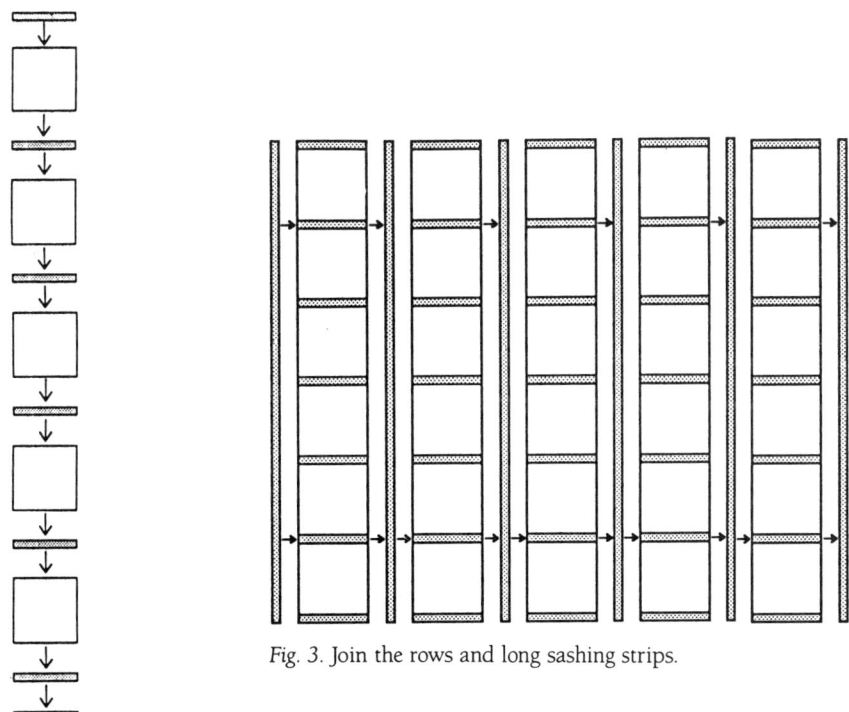

Fig. 3. Join the rows and long sashing strips.

Fig. 2. Join the blocks and sashing strips to form rows.

Fig. 4. Sew borders to top, bottom and sides.

Quilting and Finishing

Using a watercolor fabric pen, draw an inner line around each quilt block, ½″ from the seams.

Quilting should start in the center of the quilt and work to the outer border edges. Quilt around all parts of the stenciled design, including the bridges of the designs. Quilt close to all the seams on the block and border fabric; this is called quilting in the ditch. After all the quilting is completed, work the embroidery on the marked lines in each quilt block using a simple chain-stitch. The two outer rows of six quilt blocks will be worked in green, the three inner rows in red. The chain stitches are worked into the batting and should not show on the back side of the quilt. Use the quilting hoops when embroidering. Bind the quilt.

Glossary of Stenciling Terms

Acrylic paint. A permanent water-base paint used for stenciling.
Brushes. Short, stiff round-bristle brushes made specifically for stenciling, available in a variety of sizes.
Heat-set. Fabric paint must be pressed with a hot iron to make colors more permanent.
Latex paint. Paint much like acrylic paint, sometimes used for stenciling.
Mylar. Brand name for a flexible durable plastic used for stencil making.
Palette. A shallow or flat container used to hold paint.
Shellac thinner. Alcohol used for cleaning dried paint from Mylar stencils.
Stenciling prop. Any open-patterned material that can be stenciled over to create a textured look.
Stencil proof. The first trial painting for a stencil.
Stenciling shield. A scrap of cardboard or Mylar used in painting to prevent paint smudges in unwanted areas.

Glossary of Quilting Terms

Appliqué. Quilt designs cut from fabric and hand- or machine-stitched to a background fabric.
Backing. Fabric used for the back of the quilt.
Back-stitch. Used for starting and ending off the quilting stitch.
Basting stitch. 1½″- to 2″-long stitches used to hold all three layers together when assembling a quilt.
Batting. Cotton, wool or polyester fibers used for the filling of a quilt.
Binding. Usually a 3″-wide strip of fabric used to finish the raw edges of a quilt.
Block. A fabric shape, either cut as one piece, or made by stitching smaller pieces together, used as a unit of a quilt.
Borders. Horizontal and vertical strips of fabric stitched to the quilt top to resemble a picture frame.
Chain stitch. Decorative embroidery stitch.
Grain. Thread direction of the fabric—crosswise is the woof, lengthwise is the warp.
Hand quilting. A running stitch worked through the three layers of the quilt to hold it together.
Mitered corners. Binding strips folded at a 45° angle at the corners of the quilt and hemmed down.
Needles. Quilting needles, called "betweens," are available in sizes 7–10. The larger the number, the smaller the needle.
Patchwork. Fabric pieces stitched together to form a quilt top.
Pieced. Shapes of fabric stitched together.
Pins. Special quilting straight pins are 1¾″ long.
Quilting frame. Long rails suspended on a floor stand, enabling a full quilt to be stretched for quilting.
Quilting hoop. Oval or circular wood hoop, with an adjustable screw; also comes with floor stands.
Quilt top. The decorated or "right side" of the quilt; there are two kinds, whole-cloth or patchwork.
Rotary cutter. Round fabric cutter; requires a special cutting base.
Sashing. Fabric strips stitched around a quilt block or blocks; also known as lattice strips or mullion strips.
Set. A method of assembling the parts of a patchwork quilt top.
Template. A pattern shape used for marking and cutting pieces of fabric; also used for marking quilting lines.
Thimble. Finger protection from the quilting needle—to be a good quilter, you must use one.
Thread. Cotton-covered polyester is good for hand quilting.
Tied or Tufted. Quilts held together with knotted pieces of yarn.
Waffle quilting. Quilting stitches worked in a crisscross design, either squares or diamonds.
Whole-cloth. One large piece of fabric, sometimes with pieced borders.

Metric Conversion Chart

CONVERTING INCHES TO CENTIMETERS AND YARDS TO METERS

mm — millimeters   cm — centimeters   m — meters

INCHES INTO MILLIMETERS AND CENTIMETERS
(Slightly rounded off for convenience)

inches	mm		cm	inches	cm	inches	cm	inches	cm
⅛	3mm			5	12.5	21	53.5	38	96.5
¼	6mm			5½	14	22	56	39	99
⅜	10mm	or	1cm	6	15	23	58.5	40	101.5
½	13mm	or	1.3cm	7	18	24	61	41	104
⅝	15mm	or	1.5cm	8	20.5	25	63.5	42	106.5
¾	20mm	or	2cm	9	23	26	66	43	109
⅞	22mm	or	2.2cm	10	25.5	27	68.5	44	112
1	25mm	or	2.5cm	11	28	28	71	45	114.5
1¼	32mm	or	3.2cm	12	30.5	29	73.5	46	117
1½	38mm	or	3.8cm	13	33	30	76	47	119.5
1¾	45mm	or	4.5cm	14	35.5	31	79	48	122
2	50mm	or	5cm	15	38	32	81.5	49	124.5
2½	65mm	or	6.5cm	16	40.5	33	84	50	127
3	75mm	or	7.5cm	17	43	34	86.5		
3½	90mm	or	9cm	18	46	35	89		
4	100mm	or	10cm	19	48.5	36	91.5		
4½	115mm	or	11.5cm	20	51	37	94		

YARDS TO METERS
(Slightly rounded off for convenience)

yards	meters	yards	meters	yards	meters	yards	meters	yards	meters
⅛	0.15	2⅛	1.95	4⅛	3.80	6⅛	5.60	8⅛	7.45
¼	0.25	2¼	2.10	4¼	3.90	6¼	5.75	8¼	7.55
⅜	0.35	2⅜	2.20	4⅜	4.00	6⅜	5.85	8⅜	7.70
½	0.50	2½	2.30	4½	4.15	6½	5.95	8½	7.80
⅝	0.60	2⅝	2.40	4⅝	4.25	6⅝	6.10	8⅝	7.90
¾	0.70	2¾	2.55	4¾	4.35	6¾	6.20	8¾	8.00
⅞	0.80	2⅞	2.65	4⅞	4.50	6⅞	6.30	8⅞	8.15
1	0.95	3	2.75	5	4.60	7	6.40	9	8.25
1⅛	1.05	3⅛	2.90	5⅛	4.70	7⅛	6.55	9⅛	8.35
1¼	1.15	3¼	3.00	5¼	4.80	7¼	6.65	9¼	8.50
1⅜	1.30	3⅜	3.10	5⅜	4.95	7⅜	6.75	9⅜	8.60
1½	1.40	3½	3.20	5½	5.05	7½	6.90	9½	8.70
1⅝	1.50	3⅝	3.35	5⅝	5.15	7⅝	7.00	9⅝	8.80
1¾	1.60	3¾	3.45	5¾	5.30	7¾	7.10	9¾	8.95
1⅞	1.75	3⅞	3.55	5⅞	5.40	7⅞	7.20	9⅞	9.05
2	1.85	4	3.70	6	5.50	8	7.35	10	9.15

AVAILABLE FABRIC WIDTHS

25″	65cm	50″	127cm
27″	70cm	54″/56″	140cm
35″/36″	90cm	58″/60″	150cm
39″	100cm	68″/70″	175cm
44″/45″	115cm	72″	180cm
48″	122cm		

AVAILABLE ZIPPER LENGTHS

4″	10cm	10″	25cm	22″	55cm
5″	12cm	12″	30cm	24″	60cm
6″	15cm	14″	35cm	26″	65cm
7″	18cm	16″	40cm	28″	70cm
8″	20cm	18″	45cm	30″	75cm
9″	22cm	20″	50cm		

Stencils

2/3

1 stencil

A is for apple
2 stencils

1—"A," center apple and stems
2—side apples and leaves

B is for boat
3 stencils

1—"B" and waves
2—sails
3—hull and flag

C is for cat

2 stencils

1—"C," face and ears
2—top of head, features and outline of body

After the outline of body has been painted, shade in the body.

4/5

1 stencil

D is for duck

3 stencils

E is for eyes, ears and earrings
2 stencils

1—"E," eyes and earrings
2—outline of face and hair, ears, eyelashes and pupils

After the outline of the hair has been painted, shade in the hair freehand. Shade the cheeks freehand.

F is for flower
1 stencil

Shade in the center of the large leaves and the tops of the stem sections after the stem and leaves are stenciled.

G is for go
2 stencils

1—"G" and lights
2—frame and "o"

"O" is stenciled over the light.

H is for house
3 stencils

1—"H" and house
2—roof, chimney, eaves and windows
3—trees, grass and door

I is for Indian
2 stencils

1—"I," feathers, headband and lower face markings
2—hair, features and upper face markings

Stencil the lower part of each feather one color, then, without moving the stencil, stencil the upper part a different color.

J is for jack-o'-lantern
2 stencils

1—pumpkin
2—"J," stem, eyes, nose and mouth

Features are stenciled over the pumpkin.

K is for kite
2 stencils

1—kite and half of tail
2—"K," string and other half of tail

The string is stenciled over the kite.

L is for leaf
1 stencil

M is for man in the moon

2 stencils

1—moon and star
2—"M," mouth and eye

Add dot in eye freehand.

N is for no
1 stencil

For a shadow effect, move the stencil slightly and re-stencil the words in a contrasting color.

O is for owl

3 stencils

1—"O," wings, outline of body, top of head, feet, nose and tufts above eyes
2—outer eyes
3—feathers on chest and pupils

Shade in chest after wings and outline of body are stenciled, then stencil the pupils and the feathers on the chest.

P is for pineapple
2 stencils

1—pineapple "eyes"
2—"P," leaves at top and bottom

Shade in pineapple after the eyes and leaves are stenciled. This shading is worked over the eyes.

Q is for queen

3 stencils

1—"Q," crown, lips and bow
2—Outer collar and "jewels" in crown
3—Inner collar, hair, eyes, eyebrows and nose

Shade cheeks freehand.

R is for rabbit
1 stencil

S is for Santa
3 stencils

1—"S," holly leaves, face and trousers
2—nose, hat and shirt
3—eyes, suspenders, mittens and boots

T is for teddy bear

2 stencils

1—"T," eyes and vest
2—bear, nose, mouth, buttons and heart

U is for umbrella
3 stencils

1—"U," raincoat and water
2—top of umbrella, mitten and boots
3—umbrella and handle

V is for valentine
1 stencil

Add words with a waterproof permanent marker.

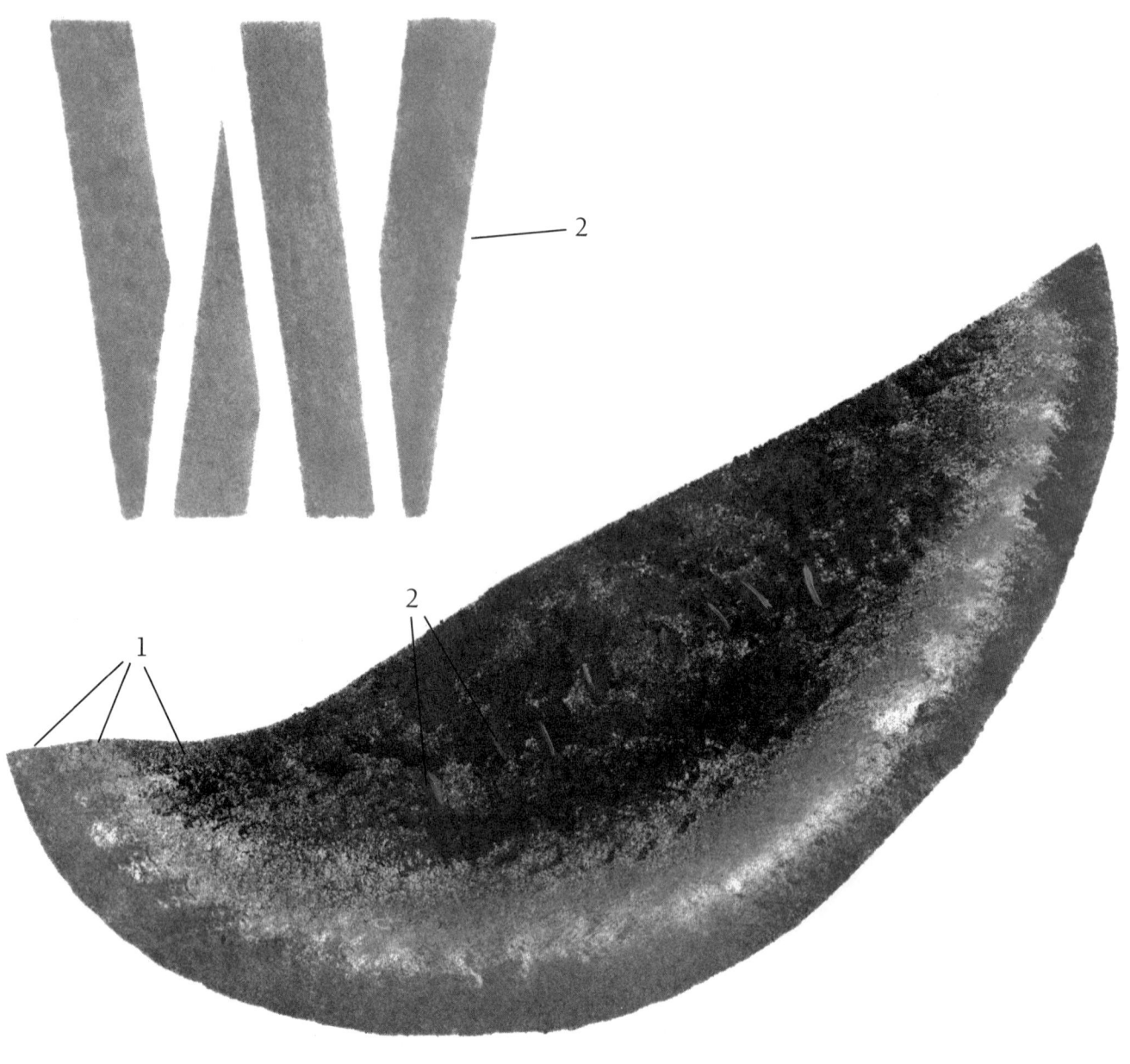

W is for watermelon
2 stencils

1—watermelon
2—"W" and seeds

To stencil the watermelon rind, work the brush off the lower edge of the stencil into the opening. Stencil a lighter color next to the rind, then shade in the rest of the watermelon.

6/7

1 stencil

X is for ?

1 stencil

Trace the inner edge of the circle and the "X" to the stencil material. Cut out the circle and the "X"; discard the rest of the stencil material. Center the circle on the block and stencil the "X." To stencil the circular frame, hold the circle firmly and work the brush off the edge. Repeat all the way around. This is called reverse or negative stenciling.

Y is for yes
1 stencil

For a shadow effect, move the stencil slightly and re-stencil the words in a contrasting color.

Z is for ?

1 stencil

Trace the inner edge of the circle and the "Z" to the stencil material. Cut out the circle and the "Z"; discard the rest of the stencil material. Center the circle on the block and stencil the "Z." To stencil the circular frame, hold the circle firmly and work the brush off the edge. Repeat all the way around. This is called reverse or negative stenciling.

8/9

1 stencil

About the Author

Marie Sturmer is a retired art teacher. Through the years, her many lesson plans included a variety of unique approaches to stencil painting.

Her formal art training began at Cranbrook Academy of Art in Bloomfield Hills, Michigan. She later earned a BA with a secondary teaching certificate from Alma College and an MFA with a major in watercolor painting from Wayne State University, both located in Michigan.

Marie is the author of two previous quilting books, *Stenciled Quilts: Techniques, Patterns and Projects*, published by Dover Publications, Inc., New York, and *Stenciled Quilts for Christmas*, published by the American Quilter's Society, Paducah, Kentucky.

As a member of the Stencil Artisans League, Inc., Norcross, GA, Marie has earned the title of Certified Stenciler and Certified Stenciling Teacher.

The Artistree Studio situated on the shores of West Grand Traverse Bay, north of Traverse City, Michigan, is the home of Marie's quilting and stenciling activities.